AF454102

SUSTAINABLE LIVING

-a magical journey

ISBN 978-91-987081-4-1

Photos by Modesty Sofronenkoff

To the beat of the drum

I went to the Spirits with my question

–How can we find ways

to sustainable living

and the power to walk them?

A wild mustang mare came to meet me.

She took me on her back and we flew away

over the great open fields

heading towards the hills at the horizon

–where the Earth meets the Sky.

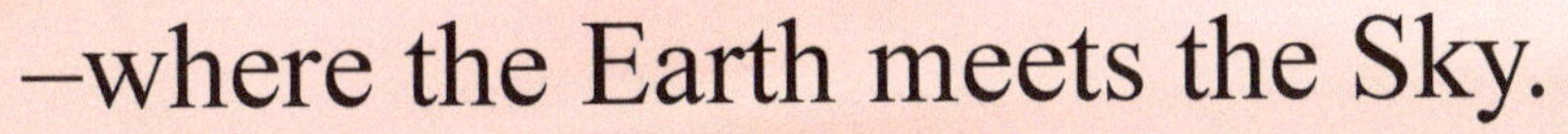

Her mane and my hair
were blended by the wind

and then came the words:

Only those

who feel the Wind in their hair

and see the beauty of the great open

wild landscapes

love the Earth as she is.

Through the Heart

we get the knowledge we need

to love and respect
the world as she is.

We who love the Water

don't want to own her

but hold her clear and clean.

We who love the Wind

don't want to pollute him

but feel gratitude

because of the refreshing

power he gives.

We who love the Sun

and see what he gives and does

understand the delicate balance

between life and destruction

and take on our responsibility.

We who love the Earth

will care for her

not own

not rape nor destroy.

We are filled with gratitude

for the beauty

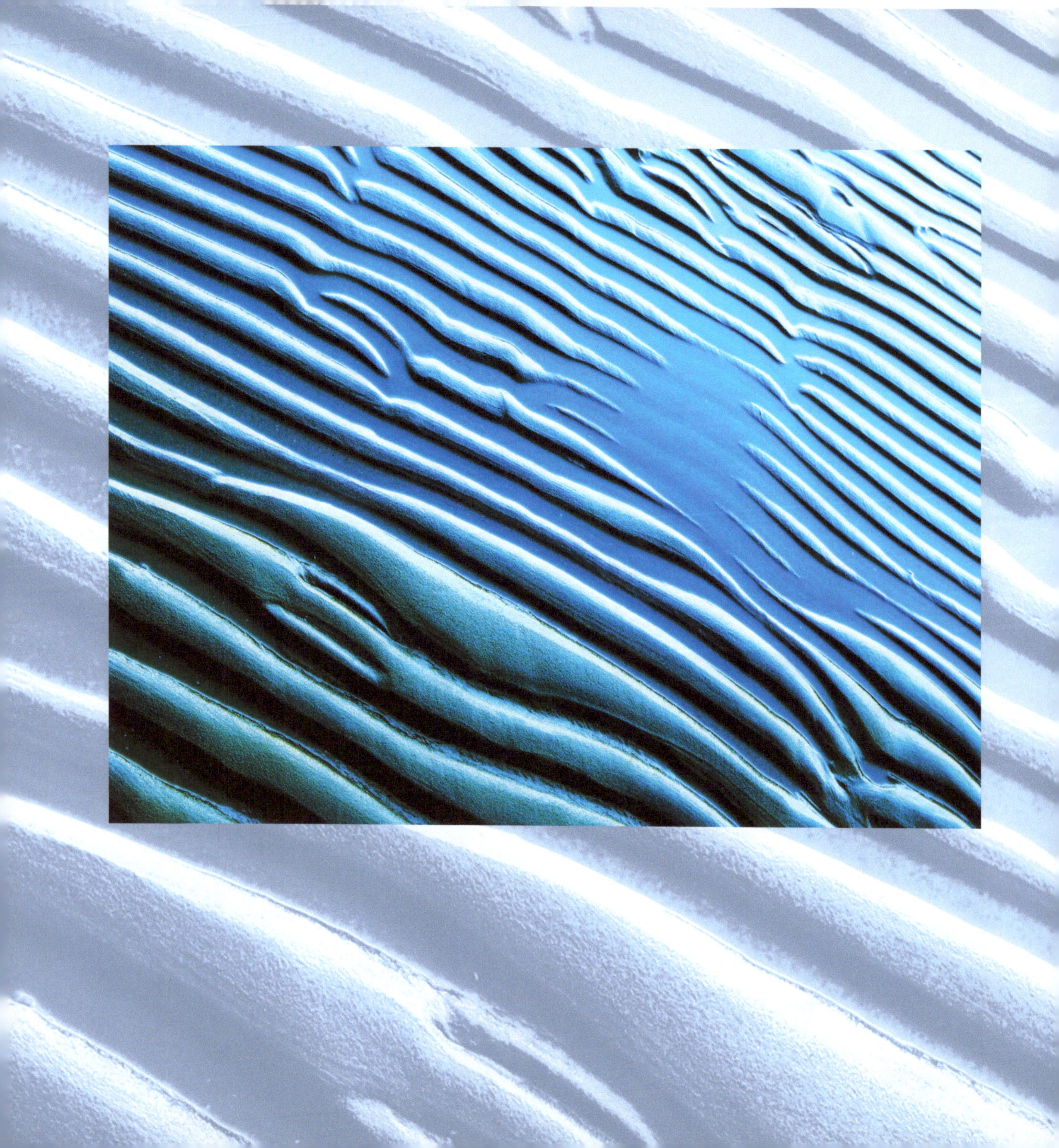

of the fine balance

and rhythm

that we now learn to keep.

–Thank You!

Sustainable Living

To the beat of the drum

I went to the Spirits with my question

–How can we find ways

to sustainable living

and the power to walk them?

A wild mustang mare came to meet me

she took me on her back and we flew away

over the great open fields

heading towards the hills at the horizon

–where the Earth meets the Sky.

Her mane and my hair were blended by the wind

and then came the words:

Only those

who feel the Wind in their hair

and see the beauty of the great open

wild landscapes

love the Earth as she is.

Through the Heart

we get the knowledge we need

to love and respect

the world as she is.

We who love the Water

don't want to own her

but hold her clear and clean.

We who love the Wind

don't want to pollute him

but feel gratitude

because of the refreshing power he gives.

We who love the Sun

and see what he gives and does

understand the delicate balance

between life and destruction

and take on our responsibility.

We who love the Earth

will care for her

not own

not rape nor destroy.

We are filled with gratitude

for the beauty

of the fine balance

and rhythm

that we now learn to keep.

–Thank You!

All photos are taken in the south of Sweden by Modesty Sofronekoff,
more of her work is to be found at: www.modestyspictures.se

Anna-Carin Martensson is living in Sweden where she works as a teacher, artist, healer and writer, more of her work is to be found at: www.spiritroad.se

We donate 10 % of the profit from the selling of this book to Greenpeace.
More soulful books at: www.spiritroad.se

www.ingramcontent.com/pod-product-compliance
Lightning Source LLC
LaVergne TN
LVHW070025220726
843527LV00015B/367